COAC... ~~DAVID'S TIME~~ TESTED TIPS ON ALL THINGS BOXING

COACH DAVID'S TIME TESTED TIPS ON ALL THINGS BOXING

Tips on Coaching, Technique, and Training

DAVID BERMUDEZ

First Printing: 2016

www.Fisticuffsboxing.net

This is dedicated to one of the greatest students, friends, and human beings I have ever known...

Sifu Nicolo Noche
4th Degree Black Belt in Macalolooy Kajukenbo

March 21, 1981 - November 15, 2016

I could not have done this without those who have supported me throughout the years in my boxing journey. Thank you Michael Dapper for dragging this insecure twelve year old kid to shadow box with you. You are the one that started it all.

Thank you to my University of Nevada Las Vegas Boxing coaches: Skipper "Saigon" Kelp, Chris Ben-Tchvtchavadze, and Frank Slaughter. I will never forget you guys. And thank you to Sigung Jeff Macalolooy for being a mentor to me long before I laced up the gloves. I appreciate you for giving this kid fresh out of college his first opportunity to coach the sweet science. Thank you Paul Rubio for allowing me to inspire, mentor, and encourage others through a sport we are so passionate about.

Thank you to everyone who gave me the privilege of teaching them the sport of boxing. I also want to thank my parents Julio and Salvadora, my brother Julio, my sister Diana, my wife Laura, and the rest of my family and friends for the never ending love and support. Thank you Dana Wilson and Albert Pinto for the patience and hard work editing this book.

I mostly want to thank my Lord and Savior Jesus Christ. Thank you for giving me the gift of learning, participating, and spreading the gospel of the sweet science.

Boxing has been a blessing. It has taught me so many life lessons and has given me the opportunity to build incredible relationships. Grit, confidence, determination, and accountability are just a few things I have picked up from the sport.

I have also had the privilege of spreading the gospel of boxing to countless people and have seen the incredibly positive transformation right before my eyes. The following are tips I have picked up throughout the years of being involved in the sweet science. I hope they assist you in providing a blueprint for partaking in one of the greatest sports in the world, boxing.

Contents

EQUIPMENT

BOXING TIP #1

GET THE PROPER EQUIPMENT

The MINIMUM pieces of equipment a boxer should have are 180 inch hand wraps, boxing shoes, and a mouthpiece. The wraps protect the hands and wrists from continuous pounding on the heavy bag and mitts. The shoes are to prevent injuries to the feet, ankles, and knees.

Last, but definitely not least, the mouthpiece is to protect the jaw and pearly whites. The mouthpiece provides protection not just from sparring, but from shadow boxing drills and/or mitt holding. Mistakes do happen. Do not be surprised if during boxing drills, you receive a punch to the mouth.

Some gyms may provide boxing gloves for heavy bag/mitt work and some may not. Bag gloves are essential in learning the sport. Down the road, sparring gear such as sparring gloves, headgear, and a groin protector will be a necessity if or when the boxer decides to step inside the ring and duke it out.

BOXING TIP #2

HEAVY BAG GLOVES

"So which boxing gloves am I supposed to get coach?" That's a question I always get asked. I recommend investing in quality boxing bag gloves. Notice I said BOXING bag gloves. Nothing against mixed martial arts or kickboxing, but the quality of the gloves are not as good for strictly boxing purposes. Several techniques are incorporated in kickboxing and mixed martial arts. Sure, punching is involved, but boxing is ALL punching.

Risk of injury increases in addition to more wear and tear on the non-boxing brand gloves.

Do not go to your local sporting good s retailer to search for quality bag gloves. Even if the gloves they sell are boxing brands, the quality is on the lower end. Order the gear directly from the website of the top boxing brands. I recommend 10-12 ounce bag gloves ONLY used to hit the mitts or heavy bags. The main boxing brands out there are Everlast, Ringside, Reyes, Winning, Rival, and Grant. The following article written by Ralph Longo provides great information on the pros and cons of gloves out there:
http://bleacherreport.com/â€¦/1286577-breaking-down-differentâ€¦
Yes, the gloves are pricier, but they are worth it.

BOXING TIP #3

HEAVY BAG AND SPARRING GLOVES

I have seen in many gyms that fighters spar with the same gloves they hit the heavy bag with. THIS IS NO BUENO! It is very dangerous to use gloves interchangeably between heavy bag/mitt work and sparring. Bag gloves are lighter than sparring gloves which heighten the risk of injury to the fighter receiving the blow when sparring. Bag gloves also harden over time, which can cause serious damage to the face. Boxing is risky business. Do not make it even riskier.

BOXING TIP #4

FITTED MOUTHPIECE

Michael Dapper
(The man who introduced me to the sweet science)

Having a mouthpiece is THE most important piece of equipment you own in ANY sport, especially boxing. Those pearly whites are irreplaceable. But not all mouthpieces are created equal. You can go to your local sporting goods store, grab a mouthpiece off of the shelf, purchase it, boil it, stick it in your mouth, and bite down. But that mouthpiece will be bulky, uncomfortable, and in many cases, painful. You will have trouble breathing and will have a hard time talking while wearing it.

The solution is a fitted mouthpiece. Ask your dentist if they can make you one. If they cannot, ask them if they can refer you to someone that can. It may be pricier but the benefits are well worth it. The mouthpiece will fit you perfectly which will enable you to breath better while working on your craft. You r teeth will be better protected and the inconvenience factor disappears. A fitted mouthpiece will be one of the best investments you can make.

BOXING TIP #5

HAVE A TOWEL AND ATHLETIC TAPE HANDY DURING SPARRING

When a sparring session has been interrupted, the flow has been compromised. Two fighters are getting some good rounds in and all of a sudden, a shoelace comes untied or a glove comes unlaced. The coach has to stop the action so the fighter will not trip and fall. Or a fighter gets in a good right hand and a nosebleed starts. The coaches are now scrambling for paper towels to stop the excess bleeding and cleanup.

All of this ruins the tempo of the sparring session. Bloody noses and cuts happen. It's boxing. Do your best to lessen the inconvenience with the right equipment by taping the gloves and shoelaces with athletic tape and always have a towel handy.

BOXING TIP #6

VASELINE

Vaseline is one of the most utilized and important things you can use in boxing. It can prevent cuts and help the punches you sustain slip off your face, preventing substantial damage. It can also help prevent nose bleeds by rubbing the vaseline inside of the nose, providing moisture. A fighter should put vaseline above and underneath the eyes, nose, lips, and headgear. If the fighter is allergic, use an alternative. I have even seen trainers rub vaseline on headgear and gloves just prior to sparring. So rub away and protect yourself at all times!

TECHNIQUE

BOXING TIP #7

KEEP THAT BOXING STANCE LOW, BALANCED, AND GROUNDED

Everything in boxing comes back to your stance. Whether it is balance, defense, or how hard your punches are, i t is all determined by your stance. Keep those elbows in, chin down, and hands up. Stay low and do not stand up straight. Standing up straight causes your balance to be thrown off and takes the power out of your punches. Keep your feet shoulder width apart and your knees slightly bent so when your opponent tries to push you with a lame punch, you will not be caught off balance.

Staying low with your feet spread apart will also give your punches an incredible amount of leverage and torque. Staying low will also help by not exposing your chin and/or rib cage. Keep those elbows in to protect yourself against debilitating body shots. All of these benefits come from something as simple as your boxing stance.

BOXING TIP #8

KEEP YOUR HANDS UP, CHIN DOWN, AND ELBOWS IN

The bread and butter of boxing is a proper stance. Beginners and even some experienced boxers sometimes negate the importance of a proper stance. DO NOT drop your hands. Keep that lead hand eye level, and that rear hand next to your chin. The great Olympic boxing coach Candelario Lopez, prompts his boxers to "talk on the phone" when he sees the rear hand dropping.

Always keep that chin tucked in. I call the chin the "Red button." Bad things happen if you push the red button. If you get clipped directly on the red button, a knock down or knockout will most likely occur.

Last, DO NOT "build a house." DO NOT hold your hands up high and flare your elbows out, exposing your rib cage. BAD THINGS WILL HAPPEN. If you get caught with a good body shot, you are going to wish you got caught in the chin instead.

Remember when you are boxing your opponent. Talk on the phone while protecting that red button. And definitely do not build him a house. It will likely come crashing down.

BOXING TIP #9

DO NOT SQUARE YOUR SHOULDERS

When in your boxing stance, do not square your shoulders, exposing your whole body in front of your opponent. You are ripe to get hit from all angles. Make it hard for your opponent and turn your shoulders and torso perpendicular. So instead of having your shoulders go from "east to west," make them "north and south." You are only exposing half of your body to your opponent, making it a lot harder to get clean shots on you.

BOXING TIP #10

BRING YOUR HANDS BACK TO YOUR FACE

When in a boxing stance, your hands should be up, elbows in, with your chin down. Your hands should stay up at all times, ready to strike or block in an instant. When it is time to throw punches, your hands should come back to your face where they were originally. Do not lower you r hands then throw a punch, or punch and bring the hands down below your chin. Your opponent could time you in the moment before or after your punch.

This mistake is most prevalent when fatigue sets in. Your gloves get heavier and heavier in the later rounds. It is a lot harder being as technically sound in the eighth round than in the first. Be disciplined, stay focused, and bring those hands back to your face!

BOXING TIP #11

EXTEND YOUR ARMS ALL OF THE WAY OUT

When shadowboxing, hitting the heavy bag, or sparring, arm extension is one of the most important things you can do when landing a blow. Do not just punch your target, punch THROUGH it. Do not pull your punches. Extend your arms all of the way out. Punching through your target maximizes the power in your punches. It is hard enough landing clean and effective punches to begin with. When you do, make the most of it, and give your opponent the full brunt of the blow!

BOXING TIP #12

JAB FROM THE LEVEL OF YOUR FACE

Many boxers like to hold their lead hand close to their face and then shoot the jab out. DO NOT DO THAT. Hold that lead hand about one foot in front of your face at the eye level and then shoot out the jab as fast as you can.

Coach Skipper "Saigon" Kelp
Fightcapital.com

It is harder for your opponent to see the jab coming since the distance has been cut significantly. If you hold your jab below your chin or close to your face, it will be a lot easier for your opponent to see the jab coming. They can slip, parry, and/or counter over the top of the jab.

Check out this video where Hall of Famer Lennox Lewis teaches the current WBC Heavyweight Champion, Deontay Wilder the proper way to throw a jab. Nobody else in the Heavyweight Division, other than Larry Holmes, jabbed better!

https://www.youtube.com/watch?v=MPJMn7izjOM

BOXING TIP #13

DO NOT PAW

When throwing the jab, shoot the arm straight out with your two lead knuckles striking your target. Do not bend the wrist up, striking the target with the inside portion of the hand, resembling a cat hitting something with its paw. It is not only ineffective it will increase the risk of injury to the wrist.

BOXING TIP #14

DO NOT CROSS YOUR FEET

One of the most underrated techniques in boxing is footwork. The sport is not all about two athletes standing in front of one another going toe to toe. It is very important to be balanced, feet shoulder width apart, with a solid foundation.

If you want to move left in your boxing stance, move your left foot first and follow it up with your right foot. When moving to the right, move your right foot first and follow it up with the left foot. If you want to go forward, move your front foot first and follow it up with your back foot. And if you want to move backwards, move your back foot first and follow up with your front foot.

Keep your feet separated and DO NOT CROSS YOUR FEET. If you cross your feet and get hit by a punch, you will trip on your own feet and fall down on the canvas. That will be scored as a knock down and you are automatically down on the scorecards. Be balanced and disciplined and keep that footwork intact.

BOXING TIP #15

STEP ON THE BUG

When throwing a punch from your right or left hand (depending on your stance), footwork is of the utmost importance. You have to be in the proper stance with your hands up, chin down, elbows in, knees bent, and slightly on the balls of your feet. When throwing the rear hand, you have to turn your hips while fully extending the elbow.

When turning the hips, you also have to "step on the bug" or twist your back foot on its ball, like you are stepping on a bug. When you "step on the bug," you get the maximum power, torque, and impact of the punch. Stepping on a bug will make the biggest difference on whether the punch is an ineffective "arm punch," a clean effective blow, or a blistering knockout.

SPARRING

BOXING TIP #16

SPAR BETTER FIGHTERS

Sure, there are many benefits to sparring fighters with less ability and/or experience than you. You can try new things and work on more speed than power. But it will not get you better as fast as sparring fighters who are better than you. You learn so much more swapping punches with more experienced fighters. They expose your mistakes and force you to correct them. They can also critique you and give good advice. The sparring sessions can be a painful experience, but the benefits are worth it.

BOXING TIP #17

SPAR AS MANY PEOPLE AS YOU CAN

Whether it is a boxing show in front of a large crowd or getting together with fighters at another gym, leave the comfort of your facility, and get out and get that experience. Everyone has a different skill level, style, and/or physical makeup. Spar the fighter with five fights, ten fights, or fifty fights. Fight the tall/skinny fighter and the short/ stocky fighter. Fight the Orthodox fighter and the southpaw. Fight the boxer and the brawler. Fighting different styles gives you a fresh look and makes you better and well rounded.

BOXING TIP #18

DO NOT FINISH YOUR SPARRING PARTNER

It gets really competitive and intense when two boxers are going at it in the ring, especially when they do not know one another. When both boxers are mixing it up, a good shot will eventually land, hurting one of the fighters, knocking him/her off balance from the blow. When this occurs, DO NOT go for the knockout.

Typically when two fighters from different gyms spar, both are getting ready for competition in the near future. The last thing a boxer wants to do is get injured right before a fight. Treat sparring sessions like sparring sessions and not a fight. Save going for the knockout for the actual fight. Think of it as "partner preservation."

BOXING TIP #19

DO NOT "TRAIN TO SPAR"

A very common excuse I have heard in the boxing world for not sparring is, "I'm out of shape." I have also heard, "Let me train first so I can get ready for sparring. SPARRING IS NOT A FIGHT. Sparring is when you get tested, gauge where you are, and a time to evaluate your stamina and technique. It is not some special competition where you have to "train" or "get ready for." In many cases, sparring is the best way to work off the ring rust to get you better prepared. So do not delay sparring. Lace up the gloves and get in the ring!

BOXING TIP #20

REST FROM SPARRING

More is not always better. It does not matter whether it is on the track, pool, or weight room. Over training is not only counterproductive, it is a cause for concern. The same goes for sparring. First and foremost, it is not healthy to receive repeated blows to the head. But to receive them day after day after day is DEFINITELY not healthy.

Injuries and serious concussions are more likely to occur if sparring is done too frequently, especially if the body is not getting enough rest. Get good quality sparring three to four times a week and limit your rounds when getting ready for a fight. In between your sparring sessions, REST THE BODY. If you do not, the fight you are training for is over before it begins.

BOXING TACTICS

Coach Chris Ben-Tchvtchavadze

BOXING TIP #21

STICK TO THE BASICS

I see fighters spending a lot of time trying different kinds of "advanced" punches and/or techniques. I see boxers trying the "Philly" defense or the "Check" hook when they are clearly not proficient at the basics. I have nothing against trying new things, but when it becomes the focus, it can be detrimental. There is nothing like a tight defense, stiff jab, solid right hand, and a good pivot to a crisp left hook. World Champions like Alexis Arguello, Glen Johnson, Julio Cesar Chavez, Ronald "Winky" Wright, and Felix Trinidad were not the fastest or flashiest boxers. But they were masters of the basics.

BOXING TIP #22

MAKE SHADOW BOXING REALISTIC

I often see boxers "going through the motions" when shadow boxing. The punches are slow, not very crisp, and one punch at a time. Many treat shadow boxing as a warm up. You know what they say, "Train how you fight." Shadow boxing is no exception. Make it realistic. Imagine an opponent in front of you. Imagine circling around your opponent or backing your opponent into the corner. Imagine the crowd yelling and screaming. The more realistic it is, the harder you work, and the less of a shock is experienced when you are in the ring competing.

BOXING TIP #23

BE DELIBERATE IN THE POCKET

When fighting on the inside (toe to toe at close proximity) stay in a good boxing stance with a solid foundation underneath you. Do not raise your stance or shuffle your feet to the side while engaging your opponent or while your opponent is engaging you. If your stance deteriorates, it opens opportunities for your opponent to hit you. Be confident in the pocket. Get ready to pivot your feet, block and counter, and slam those combinations into your opponent's head and body.

BOXING TIP #24

DO NOT BE A METRONOME

According to Wikipedia, a metronome is:

"...device that produces regular, metrical ticks (beats, clicks)-settable in beats per minute. These ticks represent a fixed, regular aural pulse;"

Every time I see a boxer repeat the same pace or "beat" when hitting the heavy bag, hitting the mitts, or sparring, I say, "Don't be a metronome!" Always mix up your tempo when engaging. Do not be predictable and let your opponent see you coming. NEVER keep the same pace when throwing punches. It is easy for a counter punch to be set up when you or your opponent are doing the same thing over and over again. Mix up the combinations and pace. If not, you could get caught with a devastating blow.

BOXING TIP #25

DO SOMETHING AFTER A COMBINATION

After throwing a crisp combination, fighters tend to admire their work. They land a few hard shots, get excited, and freeze in front of the opponent, thinking they got him/her nailed. In boxing, this is often not the case. In boxing, "A hurt man is a dangerous man."

Just because you land a great combination, daze your opponent, or even score a knockdown does not mean the fight is over. Many times your opponent comes back stronger because he/she is on the brink of getting defeated or seriously hurt. After landing a good combination, do not just stand there. DO SOMETHING. Whether it is moving your head, stepping to the side, or circling, always do something. If not, you may be the one that is going down for the count.

BOXING TIP #26

THROW BODY SHOTS

Body shots are one of the most under used punches in boxing. Many fighters disregard them in the amateurs because they feel they will not be given credit for them during competition. In addition many fighters are not comfortable throwing body shots, thinking it will open them up to be countered easily. Many fighters also believe body shots will not do damage. I am here to tell you that body shots are one of the most devastating blows you can throw in ANY combat sport.

Body shots are extremely painful when placed just below the ribcage or the solar plexus. After a perfectly placed body shot, you can almost guarantee your opponent will not be getting off the canvas. Throw body shots from all angles. Go to the head then body or body then head. Confuse your opponent and keep him guessing. Body shots are not only devastating, they will add to your arsenal in getting that W.

[QUICK STORY]

I remember regularly sparring top notch amateur and professional boxer Anthony "The Aztec Warrior" Martinez. He was one of the most devastating body punchers I have ever had the privilege of working with. He dropped me with several body shots throughout my time training with him.

Sigung Jeff Macalolooy
Dragonsdenmma.com

I remember one day my trainer Chris Ben-Tchvtchavadze walked over to me after I got up off the canvas after sparring Anthony. Anthony had dropped me with a devastating body shot. Chris asked me, "So what did you learn?" I told him that I should have dropped my elbow to block the body shot. Chris said, "No. You need to throw body shots!" Unforgettable lesson indeed.

BOXING TIP #27

THROW PUNCHES IN BUNCHES

When sparring, boxers sometimes like to throw one punch at a time. The drawback is that your opponent may block or slip and/or counter your shots by easily timing your one punch. If you throw punches in bunches, you may not land all of the punches, but you may land one or two of them. You will also disrupt the timing and make it harder for your opponent to block all of the shots. So throw three, four, or even five punch combinations. Good luck to your opponent in trying to defend all of them.

BOXING TIP #28

BE A MATADOR

Boxing is a brutal sport. The reaction to when someone puts the pressure on you is either "flight or fight." You back off and run for the hills or you want to hit your opponent as hard as you can. We as fighters can get caught up in the "fight." When somebody engages you, you want to meet them half way, like two freight trains colliding with one another. Well, there's an easier way to put your opponent on the canvas. Be a "matador."

Step to the side as your opponent is charging you, circle, and then box! Why make the fight harder by colliding with your opponent and going toe to toe? Why make it a war? Circle, pick your punches, and finish your opponent. All you have to say is "olé" AND THEN handle business!

BOXING TIP #29

DO NOT LOOP YOUR PUNCHES

You will hear boxing coaches say, "Keep your punches straight" or "Shorten up your punches." Those are prompts to not widen or loop your punches. The shortest distance from A to B is a straight line. Often times due to poor technique or fatigue, you will see boxers throw looping or wide shots in an attempt to land a hard punch. That can have dire consequences because it makes you vulnerable to getting caught or knocked out. The following is a video of the great Floyd Mayweather Jr knocking out World Champion Ricky Hatton. It displays what can occur if you loop your punches and what can happen if you shorten up your punches.

https://www.youtube.com/watch?v=AkgRfQ65FNY

DO NOT loop your punches. Keep those punches short, crisp, and tight so you can get the knockout.

BOXING TIP #30

MOVE YOUR HEAD

It is harder to hit a moving target than a still one. That is how Joe Frazier was able to be the first man to beat Muhammad Ali. He constantly moved his head, slipping and ducking those hard lefts and rights that were coming at him from all angles while moving forward. Do not make it easier for your opponent by leaving a stationary target in front of him/her. Head movement is also a great way to set up counters with hard shots of your own. You may not slip and duck all of the punches coming at you, but you sure will make your opponent miss a lot of them. As the late great Sifu Noche would said, "Make him miss, make him pa y!"

BOXING TIP #31

DO NOT LOAD UP

When you are boxing it is not necessary to "load up" on your punches or attempt to throw every punch as hard as you can. When you are throwing punches, vary the tempo and power of your punches. It not only saves you a ton of energy, it will surprise your opponent when you land the hard shot. It keeps them on their toes and gives you a psychological edge after they get hit by a powerful shot they did not expect.

BOXING TIP #32

LISTEN TO YOUR TRAINER

Your trainer can see things you cannot. Whether you are shadow boxing, hitting the heavy bag, doing mitt work, or sparring, your trainer will always see things you can do better a lot faster than you can. A good trainer should correct you AS SOON a mistake is made. If you do not have a bond with your trainer, trust your trainer, or feel he or she is incompetent, FIND ANOTHER TRAINER. There are plenty of them out there to teach you the ins and outs of the sweet science.

TRAINING

BOXING TIP #33

START BOXING

"Let me train first and work my way into the boxing gym." It surprises me how many times I have heard this as a reason why people do not start boxing. I understand it is a sport that pushes someone out of their comfort zone if they have never done it before. It can be intimidating, and in many cases, scary.

Boxing is one of the best exercise programs EVER. You do not need to start with sparring twelve rounds in the ring. You have to crawl before you learn how to walk. You need to learn how to wrap your hands, footwork, a good boxing stance, and how to throw a proper jab.

If you need to take a boxing class with a friend, DO IT. If you need to watch a few boxing sessions in order to lessen the intimidation factor, DO IT. Do not wait another day that will inhibit you in lacing up the gloves and partaking in one of the greatest sports in the world, boxing.

BOXING TIP #34

FLEXIBILITY, STRENGTH, AND CARDIO

A boxer learns really fast that just going to the boxing gym will simply not cut it if competition is looming. There is more to boxing than just hitting the gym and going home. Working on flexibility, strength, and cardio is of the utmost importance. You cannot spar multiple rounds without getting in cardio, which can consist of running, biking, elliptical, swimming, or any other high intensity interval training.

Strength training, which can consist of weight training, can help improve power in your punches, bone density, and injury prevention. Just be conscious of how much weight your are pushing (refer to Boxing Tip #44).

Flexibility helps prevent injury and helps with mobility. As Muhammad Ali said, you can "float like a butterfly and sting like a bee" a lot easier when your arms and legs are loosened up and ready to tee off on your opponent, throwing punches in bunches.

Paul Rubio
Elitetrainingca.com

I will never forget what my Coach Skipper "Saigon" told me years ago after sparring several rounds in the gym. "If you are in shape, nobody can beat you." To this day I repeat that to myself and my fighters.

BOXING TIP #35

BE A GOOD DRILL PARTNER

When conducting boxing drills, some fighters like to go easy and not exert themselves too much. They treat the drill as if it is a warm up exercise. BIG NO NO. You are not only cheating yourself, you are cheating your drill partner. Whether you are shadow boxing, holding mitts, or sparring, treat every drill as if it is real. Push your partner. Motivate him. Make him keep his hands up. Make him move his feet. Force him to perform. If you don't, your partner will not step up in real competition.

BOXING TIP #36

BREATHE AFTER YOU PUNCH

Whether shadow boxing, working the heavy bag, or sparring, many people that start boxing hold their breath after throwing a punch. This increases fatigue, which means you get tired a lot quicker, and your punches are not as hard and crisp. Exhale upon impact through the mouth and breathe in through the nose. You DO NOT want to breathe in and out through the mouth during a match or sparring. If you get caught with a punch with your mouth open, you run the risk of your jaw getting broken. Such a small thing as having an improper breathing technique could have destructive consequences.

BOXING TIP #37

WORK THE BAG, DO NOT LET THE BAG WORK YOU

When throwing lefts and rights on the heavy bag, it will start to swing back and forth at multiple angles. Instead of stopping the bag by sticking your gloves out and holding it, step to the side or circle around it, unloading lefts and rights. The combination punching will stop the bag dead in its tracks.

It is a realistic approach because your opponent is not going to stand in front of you and get pounded into submission. Your opponent is going to move at all angles, forcing YOU to use good footwork to cut him/her off or circle, in order for you to land solid shots. Stopping the heavy bag not only messes up your rhythm hitting the bag, IT IS UNREALISTIC. So work that bag, do not let it work you.

BOXING TIP #38

BE PREPARED FOR ANYTHING

It does not matter if you are fighting a boxer or puncher. Or whether you are fighting someone with more or less experience as you. Or whether you are fighting three rounds, six rounds, or twelve rounds. Like my coach Sigung Jeff Macalolooy would always say, "We want to prepare for anything."

If you are fighting a boxer, who likes to fight on the outside, have sparring partners resemble that particular style of your opponent. But once in a while, spar someone who is going to slug with you on the inside. If you are only fighting three rounds, spar six rounds to condition yourself to make three rounds seem like a vacation. If you are fighting someone who is slow but punches hard, spar someone once in a while with lightning speed. Never rely on what you THINK your opponent is going to do. You may be surprised on fight night.

BOXING TIP #39

REDUCE INTENSITY THE FINAL WEEK OF CAMP

Now that you have spent weeks on the track, in the ring, and in the weight room, you are finally ready to fight. Up to this point your body has taken a lot of punishment. You've sparred endless rounds, ran countless miles, and have done a massive amount of sit ups. The final week should be a "make weight week." Shadow box, skip rope, and play touch sparring (with very light contact). THAT'S IT.

Get a good sweat going and make sure you are close or on weight. There is no reason to keep the same intensity level the last week of camp. You have done all the work, now it is almost time to get in the ring and win the fight! So worry about making the weight and not so much on the intensity of the training.

BOXING TIP #40

TAKE TIME OFF, BUT COME BACK TO THE GYM

After a fight, boxers tend to take "time off."   T ime off ends up being weeks, then months, then years, then never coming back. I am not against taking well deserved breaks or time off, but do not disappear. Like anything else, once the routine goes by the wayside, it is hard to get back on it. Poke your head in the gym once in a while.

HABITS OUTSIDE OF THE GYM

BOXING TIP #41

ASK QUESTIONS

After a grueling workout session, many people bolt out of the gym faster than a Manny Pacquiao straight left to the jaw. I understand life has many obligations such as getting homework done, picking up the kids, starting dinner, going to work, etc. But whether it is in person or a phone call, make some time to ask your trainer how you are doing. That opens the door to a conversation about your technique, your conditioning, and/or how close you are to reaching your goals. Feedback will go a long way toward improving your boxing the next time you lace up the gloves.

BOXING TIP #42

WEIGHT MANAGEMENT

[This tip comes from the University of San Francisco Boxing Coach Angelo F. Merino]

"It is of great advantage for a fighter who makes and maintains his desired weight a week before his scheduled fight."

It is very harmful for a boxer to be immensely heavier than his desired weight class. Issues can arise such as dehydration, cramping, weakness, and vulnerability to injury if the weight is not under control. Make sure you give yourself enough time to train and make the weight. Also, stay away from fatty/fried foods. A diet like that will not give you the sufficient nourishment needed during training. Be smart and give your body the right food it needs to sustain the workouts.

BOXING TIP #43

WATCH FILM

Whether it is watching film of yourself sparring your buddy, or watching Ali vs Frazier, film can go a long way in teaching you so much about boxing. But film goes beyond watching two people engage in fisticuffs. Listen to the corner man of your favorite fighter in between rounds. Listen to the EDUCATED commentators during the fight.

Dana Wilson

Watch documentaries of your favorite fighters and how they became world champions. Watch training films, which will not only give you great ideas, but motivate you to hit the gym and reach your goals. Watch interviews, getting into your favorite fighter's mindset and keys to success. Film is such an invaluable asset.

BOXING TIP #44

GET TO KNOW THE BOXING COMMUNITY

Boxing is a small community where everyone knows one another. Get to know them. Once you start building relationships, you can ask one another for boxing advice, go to one another's gym to spar, ask another coach you trust if they can wrap your hands or corner you in a fight as a backup. Building trust and credibility with those in the boxing community creates more opportunities.

BOXING TIP #45

WEIGHTS OR NO WEIGHTS?

I have heard several boxing trainers profess that weightlifting is a big no no if you are a fighter. Many believe it will slow you down and make you stiff as a board. They say weights will give you big muscles thus not making you as graceful and will inhibit proper punching technique. I agree... kind of. If you want to lift weights and resemble Mr. Olympia, yes, it may slow you down and not make you execute your punches as fast and crisp. But most fighters do not have the time or desire to look like the winner of the Arnold Classic.

Fighters want speed, power, and agility. Weight lifting is just a piece of what fighters want. Just look how successful Mike Tyson, Evander Holyfield, Lennox Lewis, and the Klitschko brothers were. They pushed the weight and were great world champions. Weights are extremely beneficial, just do not get too "pumped up."

COMPOSURE AND ATTITUDE

BOXING TIP #46

BE CALM

Boxing is a nerve wracking sport. There is nothing like one on one combat. The only person you can depend on in the ring is yourself. Because of this, nerves are at their peak just before a fight. Breathing elevates and muscles tighten. All of this even before the bell rings, though it continues after the bell rings and throughout the fight. This completely saps your energy.

Whether you or a beginner or have been boxing most of your life, do your best to reserve as much energy as you can. Sit down. Do some slow breathing. Listen to music. Meditate. Loosen up your shoulders and back. BE CONSCIOUSLY RELAXED. You are going to need all the energy you can muster once you touch gloves.

BOXING TIP #47

GET HIT AND MOVE ON

It is very unnatural to get hit in the face. It is even more unnatural to get knocked down by a punch to the face. But if you have boxed long enough, you know it is bound to happen. If you get caught with a good shot or knocked down, do not dwell on it. Accept it and move on. Do not be discouraged. Yes, getting your bell rung or the air knocked out of you sucks. But when you get up off the canvas, say to yourself, "Ok, it's my turn now."

BOXING TIP #48

BEHAVE LIKE A WINNER

Whether in the gym or during competition, I see many fighters leaning on the ropes, bending down with their hands on their knees, or on the canvas taking a knee with their tongue hanging out of their mouth because of exhaustion. DO NOT DO THAT. Do what the great trainer Teddy Atlas said to do. "Behave like a winner."

No matter how exhausted you are, stand up tall, put your hands behind your head, breath in through the nose, out through the mouth, and catch your breath. Train yourself to do this during training because if you do not, you will resort to bad habits during competition. The judges are heavily influenced in a close fight on who behaves like a winner. Do not let something as simple as body language influence the judges on deciding an outcome to a fight.

BOXING TIP #49

SHOW GOOD SPORTSMANSHIP

Boxing is violent. Boxing is brutal. Boxing is combat. Boxing is unforgiving. But boxing is still a sport. It is not a brawl or a street fight. There are rules and regulations to the sweet science. When sparring or when competition is over, shake each other's hands and be gracious. Afterwards, go to the other coaches and shake their hands showing good sportsmanship. Act with class after partaking in one of the most beautiful sports in the world.

BOXING TIP #50

STAY HUMBLE

Do not think you are Billy Bad Ass. Do not think you know it all. There will always be someone better than you or who knows more than you, in AND out of the gym. Even if you are the greatest of all time, your days are numbered. If you cannot be humble, one day someone will humble you.

COACHING

Coaching is an art. It is a skill. Just like learning the basic fundamentals of boxing, it is something that is learned after years of experience. You need command presence, confidence, excellent communications skills, and most of all patience. The following are some tips I have picked up over the years in coaching the sweet science.

BOXING TIP #51

BE A COACH, NOT A DRILL INSTRUCTOR

I was a young active competitor when I started coaching. I always had a "fighter's mentality." I never thought about tailoring my coaching style to my audience. I did not know any better because I figured I was hired to do a job and that job was to mold fighters. BIG MISTAKE.

I barked orders like a drill instructor. I constantly picked apart everyone's technique. As a result, I turned off a lot of people. I turned off the bullied kid, the mom who wanted to get in shape, and the white collar business man who wanted to shed a few pounds. Just because people are not interested in competing does not mean they will not be a HUGE asset. They can cheer on the fighters, be outstanding drill partners, and offer advice to EVERYONE in the gym.

Know your audience. Ask about their expectations. Ask about their goals. Do not treat the soccer mom like the seventeen year old who has ten amateur fights. Ease up on the kid who wants to learn how to throw a punch but make sure you ratchet up the intensity on the gal training for her first fight. If you do not tailor to your audience, you will end up with an empty gym.

My Parents Julio and Salvadora Bermudez

BOXING TIP #52

KNOW THAT NOT EVERYONE IS A FIGHTER

When I started coaching, I anticipated training nothing but competitive boxers. I was ready to build a huge team and go to weekend tournaments with every single weight class filled. I wanted everyone to get sparring gear and go round after round in the ring. If they did not get sparring gear, oh well. They just went to the corner and hit the heavy bag by themselves.

Little did I know, the sweet science was not strictly for people who wanted to compete. I eventually learned that some want to learn technique and get in shape while some want to be the next amateur national champion. Fighters are great, but they are not the only breed of boxer.

BOXING TIP #53

DO NOT OVERWHELM YOUR STUDENTS

No matter the level of your boxers, they are going to make mistakes. EVERYONE DOES. When a boxer first starts, their feet are a mess, their hands are down, and their chin is exposed. Focus on one mistake at a time. It is useless to constantly correct each and every mistake a fighter is making at once. The boxer will get frustrated, upset, and may eventually give up. Do not overwhelm. Once they correct one mistake, have them correct the next one. Sooner or later, there will be fewer mistakes.

BOXING TIP #54

DO NOT CHANGE YOUR BOXER'S STYLE, MAKE IT BETTER

Could you imagine Mike Tyson being taught how to fight like Muhammad Ali? When coaching, pay close attention to your boxer's style. Does the boxer like to get inside, be at close range, and bang to the head and body with hooks and uppercuts? Does the boxer like to circle around the ring, popping jabs and straight rights all night long? Or is the boxer a combination of the two? Enhance the style you see. Do not try to make a pure boxer into a puncher or vice versa.

BOXING TIP #55

DO NOT HOLD MITTS STANDING IN CEMENT AND ON STILTS

So many trainers hold mitts for their boxers as if they are standing in cement with their legs straight as stilts. This type of mitt holding is not only unrealistic, it is detrimental to the boxer. Bend those knees and change your level. Move your feet front to back, left to right, and side to side. Throw some soft punches, circle around the boxer, feint, and keep him on his toes. Do not be a stationary target. If your fighter decides to spar or compete, their opponent will not stand still, so do not train them to hit a stationary target.

BOXING TIP #56

TAILOR TO YOUR AUDIENCE

Sometimes your classes will be filled with beginners and absolutely no veterans and vice versa. Coach to your audience's knowledge and ability. Tailor your training session. Let's say you planned on sparring and a bunch of beginners showed up. Instead of sparring, work on fundamentals and conditioning. If only veterans showed up, make it a sparring day instead of a fundamentals day. If there is a mix of skill level, adjust accordingly. Be flexible and tailor to who shows up to get in some work!

BOXING TIP #57

LET THEM SEE YOU IN ACTION

To coach the sweet science it is not necessary to have been a fighter. But if you have a few fights under your belt, get in the ring or get on the heavy bag and show your students how it's done! When your students watch a seasoned fighter spar or work the heavy bag, especially if it is their coach, it is invaluable. Your students learn so much watching it happen right before their eyes. Sure, watching film is beneficial, but nothing replaces the sweet science in the flesh. So lace em' up once in a while!

CONCLUSION

Whether you want to start boxing or coaching, I hope this book provided you a foundation for beginning your journey. Boxing is one of the hardest, most brutal, and unforgiving sports. At the same time, boxing is one of the most beautiful, beneficial, and life changing sports. So get out there, lace up the gloves, and have some fun!

If you have any questions or concerns, feel free to can contact me at **Fisticuffsboxing@gmail.com**. I would love to hear your thoughts. Thank you and God bless.

Sigung Macalolooy and Albert Pinto

Made in United States
North Haven, CT
11 September 2022